Romans 5 - 8

'As you'd expect, John Stott explains these challenging chapters with great clarity. He enables us to get our heads around core truths for the Christian journey and leads us into praise and thankfulness to the Jesus of the gospel.'
Hugh Palmer, Rector, All Souls, Langham Place, London

'A daily dose of Stott on Romans is the very best antidote to fear, uncertainty, sin, suffering and even death itself. A fantastic explanation of an amazing section of the Bible!'
Jonathan Lamb, former Director, Langham Preaching, and
Minister-at-Large, Keswick Ministries

30-DAY DEVOTIONAL

Romans 5 - 8

John Stott

with Elizabeth McQuoid

ivp

Keswick
Resources

FOOD
FOR THE
JOURNEY

INTER-VARSITY PRESS
36 Causton Street, London SW1P 4ST, England
Email: ivp@ivpbooks.com
Website: www.ivpbooks.com

First published 2018

British Library Cataloguing-in-Publication Data
A catalogue record for this book is available from the British Library.

ISBN: 978–1–78359–718–5
eBook ISBN: 978–1–78359–719–2

Set in Avenir 11/15 pt
Typeset in Great Britain by CRB Associates, Potterhanworth, Lincolnshire
Printed in Great Britain by CPI Group (UK) Ltd, Croydon, CR0 4YY

Preface

Can you guess how many sermons have been preached from the Keswick platform? Almost 6,500!

For over 140 years, the Convention in the English Lake District has welcomed gifted expositors from all over the world. Our archive is a treasure trove of sermons preached on every book of the Bible.

This series is an invitation to mine that treasure. It takes talks from the Bible Reading series given by well-loved Keswick speakers, past and present, and reformats them into daily devotionals. Where necessary the language has been updated but, on the whole, it is the message you would have heard had you been listening in the tent on Skiddaw Street. Each day of the devotional ends with a fresh section of application designed to help you apply God's Word to your own life and situation.

Whether you are a Convention regular or have never been to Keswick, this Food for the Journey series is a unique opportunity to study the Scriptures with a Bible teacher by your side. Each book was designed to fit in your jacket pocket or handbag so you can read it anywhere – over the breakfast table, on the commute into work or college, while you are waiting in your car, over your lunch break or in bed at night. Wherever life's journey takes you, time in God's Word is vital nourishment for your spiritual journey.

Our prayer is that these devotionals become your daily feast, a nourishing opportunity to meet with God through his Word. Read, meditate, apply and pray through the Scriptures given for each day, and allow God's truths to take root and transform your life.

If these devotionals whet your appetite for more, there is a 'For further study' section at the end of each book. You can also visit our website <www.keswickministries.org/resources> to find the full range of books, study guides, CDs, DVDs and mp3s available. Why not order an audio recording of the Bible Reading series to accompany your daily devotional?

Let the word of Christ dwell in you richly.
(Colossians 3:16, ESV)

Introduction
Romans 5 – 8

Is the gospel good news for Christians?

Too many of us behave as if the gospel were only good news for unbelievers, as if having become a Christian we have arrived, we have come to a dead end and there is no further road to travel. But that is not true! Our conversion is only the start. It is the first step on the journey of a lifetime, where the gospel profoundly affects how we think and live. It shapes how we deal with suffering, how we view our identity, how we pray, how we battle against sin, how we face opposition, where we look for security, what we devote ourselves to, what we hope for and so much more.

Paul urgently wanted the church in Rome to appreciate the gospel message and its implications for their present and future. He began his letter by setting out the need and way of justification. Justification is a legal declaration of 'not guilty'. God declares us righteous because Jesus paid the penalty for sin we deserved, when he died on the cross. Paul explained that all of us are sinners under the just judgment of God and only through the redemption that is in Jesus Christ can we be justified, by grace alone through faith alone. Then chapter 5:1 begins, 'Therefore, since we have been justified through faith . . .' (emphasis added), and Paul launches into the immense privileges that believers can enjoy both now and in eternity. Chapters 5–8 are a glorious description of what the gospel means for Christ's followers: we have peace with God (chapter 5), union with Christ (chapter 6), freedom from the law (chapter 7) and life in the Spirit (chapter 8).

This devotional is based on the seminal Bible Reading series that John Stott gave at the Keswick Convention in 1965. The text is written by Elizabeth McQuoid but reworked from John Stott's original messages. The content of the Bible Readings was revised and published under the title Men Made New in 1966. The material was further revised and published by IVP as The Message of Romans, part of the Bible Speaks Today series.

Politically, economically and socially, the world is a much different place from when John Stott first gave these talks. Many of the issues facing Christians today would not have been thought of in 1965. And yet the timeless message of the gospel has never been more relevant or needed. Now, more than ever, believers require a robust understanding of the gospel. It is much more than a ticket to glory; it lights up the way to guide you there.

The gospel is good news for you!

Day 1

Read Romans 5:1–5
Key verses: Romans 5:1–2

....

¹Therefore, since we have been justified through faith, we have peace with God through our Lord Jesus Christ, ²through whom we have gained access by faith into this grace in which we now stand. And we boast in the hope of the glory of God.

What happened when you first trusted Christ?

Paul says you were 'justified through faith'. Justification is a legal declaration of 'not guilty'. God declares us righteous because Jesus paid the penalty for sin that we deserved when he died on the cross. This momentary act leads to a permanent relationship with God, summed up by three words:

• Peace

Peace with God is the immediate effect of our justification. We were once enemies of God (verse 10) but now, because of Jesus' death on the cross and God's forgiveness, that old hostility has been dealt with.

• Grace

The continuing effect of our justification is that 'we have been allowed to enter the sphere of God's grace' (verse 2, NEB) and we are now standing in it.

• Glory

The ultimate effect of justification, for which we hope, is 'the glory of God'. In verse 2 this means heaven, since in heaven God himself is fully revealed ('glory' is God revealed). Our 'hope' is our certain confidence that we shall see and share in God's glory, so much so that we can 'boast' or rejoice in it already.

Do you see how that one-off declaration of 'not guilty' has such an impact? It covers the three phases of our salvation. In the word 'peace', we look back to the enmity which is now over. In the word 'grace', we look up to our reconciled Father in whose favour we now continue to stand. In the word 'glory', we look to our final destiny, seeing and reflecting the glory of God, which is the object of our hope or expectation.

Today reflect on what being justified means:

- Enjoy peace with God. Don't let past failures steal your joy or hinder your service. Christ's work on the cross has dealt with your sin and guilt, so don't let Satan rehearse it.
- Bask in God's grace. There is nothing you can do or need to do to earn God's approval. Because of Christ's death and your restored relationship with God, you are already enjoying God's favour. In response, live gratefully for an audience of One.
- Look forward to eternity with Christ. One day, you will reflect the Lord's glory perfectly. Until then, ask for his help to reflect him more and more in your priorities, values, actions and attitudes.

But when the kindness and love of God our Saviour appeared, he saved us, not because of righteous things we had done, but because of his mercy. He saved us through the washing of rebirth and renewal by the Holy Spirit, whom he poured out on us generously through Jesus Christ our Saviour, so that, having been justified by his grace, we might become heirs having the hope of eternal life.

(Titus 3:4–7)

Day 2

Read Romans 5:1–5
Key verses: Romans 5:3–4

···

³Not only so, but we also glory in our sufferings, because we know that suffering produces persever- ance; ⁴perseverance, character; and character, hope.

What should we expect from the Christian life? Comfort and ease until we see Jesus?

Paul is clear: we shall suffer (verse 3). These sufferings are not, strictly speaking, sickness or pain, sorrow or bereavement, but the pressures of living in a godless and hostile world. Such suffering always precedes glory (Luke 24:26; Romans 8:17). It is not that the one is the way to the other. Still less is it that we grin and bear the one in anticipation of the other. No, we 'rejoice' in both (RSV).

How can we rejoice or glory in our sufferings? Verses 3–5 explain the paradox. It is not the sufferings themselves we rejoice in as much as their beneficial results. We are not masochists who enjoy being hurt. We are not even Stoics, who grit their teeth and endure. We are Christians, who see in our sufferings the working out of a gracious divine purpose. We rejoice because of what suffering 'produces'. Look at the three stages in this process:

• Stage 1 – suffering produces perseverance

The very endurance we need in suffering is produced by it. We could not learn perseverance without suffering, because without suffering there would be nothing to persevere in.

• Stage 2 – perseverance produces character

Character is the quality of something which, or someone who, has stood the test. It is the quality that David's armour lacked, because he had not 'proved' it (1 Samuel 17:39, KJV). We can usually recognize the ripe character of one who has gone through suffering and come out triumphant.

• Stage 3 – character produces hope

The character which has a maturity born of past suffering brings a hope of future glory. Our developing Christian character is evidence that God is at work upon us and within us. And he who is maturing us through suffering will surely and safely bring us to glory.

Do you see there is an indissoluble link between sufferings and glory? The reason why, if we rejoice in hope of the glory of God, we rejoice in our sufferings also, is that our sufferings produce hope. If the hope of glory is produced by sufferings, then we rejoice in the sufferings as well as the glory; we rejoice not only in the end, but in the means which bring us there.

Are you feeling the pressure of living in a godless society? Are you suffering for being a Christian at home or at work? Will you allow this suffering to do its work in your life, to accomplish God's purpose? Will you rejoice in it?

> Consider it a sheer gift, friends, when tests and challenges come at you from all sides. You know that under pressure, your faith-life is forced into the open and shows its true colors. So don't try to get out of anything prematurely. Let it do its work so you become mature and well-developed, not deficient in any way.
>
> (James 1:2–4, MSG)

Day 3

Read Romans 5:1–5
Key verse: Romans 5:5

....

> 5 *And hope does not put us to shame, because God's love has been poured out into our hearts through the Holy Spirit, who has been given to us.*

How can we know that our hope of future glory is not wishful thinking?

Paul asserts that this 'hope will not lead to disappointment' (NLT). But how can we be sure? He gives his answer in the rest of verse 5. The solid foundation of our hope rests on the love of God. It is because God has set his love on us that we know he is going to bring us safely to glory.

We believe that we are going to persevere to the end, and we have good grounds for this confidence. As we thought about on Day 2, our confidence is partly because of the character that God is forming in us through suffering. Remember that suffering produces perseverance; perseverance, character; character, hope. The argument is that if he is sanctifying us now, he will surely glorify us later. But our confidence is chiefly because of God's love. We know we are going to see and share in the glory of God because we know God loves us and he will never let us down, never let us go.

But how do we know God loves us? Because we have an inner experience of it. Verse 5 tells us that the Holy Spirit has been given to every believer, and one of the works of the Spirit is to pour out God's love into our hearts – that is, to make us vividly and inwardly aware that God loves us. Or, as Paul expresses the same truth in chapter 8, to witness with our spirit that we are God's children and that he is our Father who loves us.

Note the tenses of the verbs in verse 5. The Holy Spirit has been given to us (aorist), a past once-for-all event; God's love has been poured out into our hearts (perfect), a past event with abiding results. The Holy Spirit was given to us when we believed. At the same time, he flooded our hearts with God's love. He still does. The flood remains; it continues. The once-given Spirit caused a permanent flood of divine love in our hearts.

Some people are shocked if we say that we know where we are going after we die. Others roll their eyes at our arrogance. Yet we can be sure we shall one day see and share in the glory of God. Not because of our performance, meaning that we have no cause for self-righteousness, but because of the steadfast love of God.

Listen to the Holy Spirit whisper this truth to your soul as you read God's Word: you are loved by God. There is no experience you will go through that will ever get in the way of God loving you (Romans 8:35, 38–39).

> Let the beloved of the LORD rest secure in him,
>> for he shields him all day long,
>> and the one the LORD loves rests between his
>>> shoulders.
> (Deuteronomy 33:12)

Day 4

Read Romans 5:6–11
Key verses: Romans 5:6–8

....

⁶You see, at just the right time, when we were still powerless, Christ died for the ungodly. ⁷Very rarely will anyone die for a righteous person, though for a good person someone might possibly dare to die. ⁸But God demonstrates his own love for us in this: while we were still sinners, Christ died for us.

No-one likes to hear someone else speaking badly of them. These verses make for very uncomfortable reading as we are described in the most unflattering terms. We are 'powerless' because we are unable to save ourselves (verse 6), 'ungodly' because we are in revolt against God's authority (verse 6), 'sinners' because we have missed the mark of God's righteousness, however hard we may have tried to aim at it (verse 8), and 'enemies' because of the hostility that exists between us and God (verse 10). What a devastating description of us in our sin. We are failures, rebels and enemies, helpless to save ourselves. Yet it is for people like us that Jesus Christ died.

We would hardly die for a righteous person (one who is coldly upright in his or her conduct), although perhaps some people would even dare to die (verse 7) for a good person (warm and attractive in his or her goodness). But God shows *his* love (the word is emphatic – his own love, his unique love) in giving Christ to die for sinners. Not for the upright, not even for the good, but for unattractive, unworthy sinners.

Do you see how much God loves us? The objective ground for believing that God loves us is historical; it is the death of his Son (verse 8). The subjective ground for believing that God loves us is experiential; it is the gift of the Spirit (verse 5).

So we know that God loves us. We know it rationally as we contemplate the cross. God gave his best for the worst. We know it intuitively as the Holy Spirit floods our hearts with a sense of it. This, then, is our assurance of final salvation.

When prayers seem to go unanswered, when you are dealing with inexplicable and difficult circumstances and God seems distant, when you look at your own sin and failings, is your default mode to doubt God's love? In those times will you turn to the cross and accept it as God's own proof of his love for you? Then ask him to flood your heart with the Holy Spirit. Let your doubts and fears be swallowed up in the steadfast love of God.

> But because of his great love for us, God, who is rich in mercy, made us alive with Christ even when we were dead in transgressions – it is by grace you have been saved.
>
> (Ephesians 2:4–5)

> This is how God showed his love among us: he sent his one and only Son into the world that we might live through him. This is love: not that we loved God, but that he loved us and sent his Son as an atoning sacrifice for our sins.
>
> (1 John 4:9–10)

Day 5

Read Romans 5:6–11
Key verses: Romans 5:9–11

....

⁹Since we have now been justified by his blood, how much more shall we be saved from God's wrath through him! ¹⁰For if, while we were God's enemies, we were reconciled to him through the death of his Son, how much more, having been reconciled, shall we be saved through his life! ¹¹Not only is this so, but we also boast in God through our Lord Jesus Christ, through whom we have now received reconciliation.

Hold fast to this truth: you will not fall by the way, you shall be glorified.

Paul continues to set out his case for our full and final salvation by using an *a fortiori*, a 'much more' argument. This is an argument from the lesser to the greater, which reaches up to a new truth by standing on the shoulders of an old one. Paul contrasts the two main stages of salvation, justification and glorification, and shows how the first is the guarantee of the second. Look how he builds his case:

• He contrasts present justification and future salvation (verse 9)

If we are already saved from God's condemnation because we are justified, surely we shall be saved from his wrath on the day of judgment?

• He contrasts how they are achieved (verse 10)

Surely the risen life of Christ in heaven will complete what the death of Christ began on earth (see Romans 8:34)?

• He contrasts who receives them (verse 10)

It was while we were enemies that we were reconciled to God by the death of Jesus. How much more will we be saved by his life now that we are reconciled to him? If God reconciled his enemies, surely he will save his friends!

Paul's argument is not sentimental optimism; it is grounded in irresistible logic. If God performed the more costly service (involving Jesus' death) for his enemies, he will surely do the easier and less costly service now that his former enemies have become his friends.

But don't only look back to justification or on to glorification. We can't always be preoccupied with the past and the future. You have a Christian life to live now. Verse 11 urges us to 'boast' or 'rejoice in God through our Lord Jesus Christ, through whom we have now received our reconciliation' (RSV). We rejoice in the hope of glory (verse 2). We rejoice in our sufferings (verse 3). But, above all, we rejoice in God himself through Jesus Christ.

Through Christ we have peace with God (verse 1). Through Christ we have obtained access into the grace in which we stand (verse 2). Through the blood of Christ we have been reconciled, and through the life of Christ we are going to be saved (verse 9). As the Apostle John said, 'From his abundance we have all received one gracious blessing after another' (John 1:16, NLT).

Today, regardless of your present circumstances or struggles, rejoice in God through Christ for all that he has done, continues to do, and will do for you.

Day 6

Read Romans 5:12–21
Key verses: Romans 5:12–14

. . . .

¹²*Therefore, just as sin entered the world through one man, and death through sin, and in this way death came to all people, because all sinned –*

¹³*To be sure, sin was in the world before the law was given, but sin is not charged against anyone's account where there is no law.* ¹⁴*Nevertheless, death reigned from the time of Adam to the time of Moses, even over those who did not sin by breaking a command, as did Adam, who is a pattern of the one to come.*

We know that our actions can have a profound effect on others. But, in the case of Jesus, how can one person's sacrifice bring *so much* blessing to *so many*?

To answer this question, Paul draws an analogy between Adam and Christ. Both Adam and Christ demonstrate the principle that *many* can be affected (for good or ill) by *one* person's deed.

Verses 12–14 concentrate on Adam. Verse 12 sums up in three stages the history of man before Christ.

1. Sin entered the world through one person.

2. Death entered the world through sin, because death is the penalty for sin.

3. Death spread to all people, because everyone sinned.

In verses 13–14, Paul explains how this present situation of universal death is due to the original transgression of one man. All people die, not because all have sinned *like* Adam, but because they have sinned *in* Adam. This is clear, Paul argues, because of what happened during the time between Adam and Moses, between the Fall and the giving of the Law. During that period, people certainly sinned, but their sin was not reckoned against them because sin is not reckoned when there is no law. Yet they still died. Paul explains that they died not because they deliberately transgressed like Adam, and died for their transgressions, but because they and the whole of humanity were involved and included in Adam, the head of the human race. It is because we sinned in Adam that we die today.

Death is the one great certainty of life. We weep and grieve, feeling the loss of family and friends intensely. In the midst of sadness, for believers, there is hope:

> For my Father's will is that everyone who looks to the Son and believes in him shall have eternal life, and I will raise them up at the last day.
> (John 6:40)

Even as we face the pain of dying or watching our loved ones die, there is comfort:

> Even though I walk
>   through the darkest valley,
> I will fear no evil,
>   for you are with me;
> your rod and your staff,
>   they comfort me.
> (Psalm 23:4)

> Death is not the end of the road; it is only a bend in the road. The road winds only through those paths through which Christ himself has gone . . . Often we say that Christ will meet us on the other side. That is true, of course, but misleading. He walks with us on this side of the curtain and then guides us through the opening. We will meet him there, because we have met him here.
> (Erwin Lutzer, *Heaven and the Afterlife*, Moody Publishers, 2016, p. 238)

Day 7

Read Romans 5:12–21
Key verses: Romans 5:15–17

....

> [15] *But the gift is not like the trespass. For if the many died by the trespass of the one man, how much more did God's grace and the gift that came by the grace of the one man, Jesus Christ, overflow to the many!* [16] *Nor can the gift of God be compared with the result of one man's sin: the judgment followed one sin and brought condemnation, but the gift followed many trespasses and brought justification.* [17] *For if, by the trespass of the one man, death reigned through that one man, how much more will those who receive God's abundant provision of grace and of the gift of righteousness reign in life through the one man, Jesus Christ!*

A pattern is an example, an indication, of what we can expect from the genuine article. Adam is described as a pattern or prototype of Christ because his actions affected many (verse 14). But there the similarities end. Paul contrasts the difference between:

• The motive behind their deeds (verse 15a)

Adam's behaviour was self-assertive, going his own way; Christ's deed was one of self-sacrifice, of free, unmerited favour.

• The effect of their deeds (verses 15b–17)

The sin of Adam brought condemnation; the work of Christ brings justification. The reign of death is due to Adam's sin; a reign of life is made possible through Christ's work.

• The nature of their deeds (verses 18–19)

What led to condemnation for all was one man's offence, and what led to justification and life for all (in Christ) was one man's righteousness. Adam disobeyed the will of God and so fell from righteousness; Christ obeyed the will of God and so fulfilled all righteousness (see Matthew 3:15; Philippians 2:8).

Looking back over these verses, we see a striking and significant contrast between Adam and Christ. As to the motive for their deeds: Adam asserted himself; Christ sacrificed himself. As to the nature of their deeds: Adam disobeyed the law; Christ obeyed it. As to the effect of their deeds: Adam's sin brought condemnation and death; Christ's righteousness brought justification and life.

So whether we are condemned or justified, alive or dead, depends on whether we belong to the old humanity initiated by Adam or the new humanity initiated by Christ. All men are in Adam, since we are in Adam by *birth*. But not all are in Christ, since we are in Christ by *faith*. In Adam by birth we are condemned and die; but if we are in Christ by faith, we are justified and live. The privileges of the justified – peace, grace and glory (Romans 5:1–2) – belong only to those who are in Christ.

There are only two types of people in the world: those who belong to the old humanity and those who belong to the new. Today, as you praise God for all the wonderful privileges that you enjoy because you belong to Christ, pray too for specific friends, family members or work colleagues who don't yet know him. Pray that God would open their eyes and grant them faith to believe. Be ready for the opportunities that God gives you to share the gospel with them.

Day 8

Read Romans 6:1–7

Key verses: Romans 6:1–3

∙∙

¹What shall we say, then? Shall we go on sinning, so that grace may increase? ²By no means! We are those who have died to sin; how can we live in it any longer? ³Or don't you know that all of us who were baptised into Christ Jesus were baptised into his death?

Why should I stop sinning if sin provides an opportunity for God to show his grace by forgiving me? Wouldn't it be better to go on sinning so that grace may increase? Romans 5:20–21 prompts this question and Paul is quick to reply: 'By no means!' He asks, 'How can we?' If the Christian life begins with a death to sin, it is ridiculous to ask if we are free to keep on sinning. How can we go on living in what we have died to?

The burning question is: in what sense have we died to sin? Paul explains this in Romans 6:1–14 and we shall unpack his argument over the next few days. He begins by explaining that we were baptized 'into Christ'. The fact that people can even think of asking whether Christians are free to sin betrays a complete lack of understanding of what a Christian is, and of what Christian baptism is. The Christian is not just a justified believer; he or she is someone who has entered into a vital, personal union with Christ, and baptism signifies this.

Again and again, the preposition employed with the verb 'to baptize' is *eis*, 'into'. In the Great Commission, the Lord said we were to baptize *into* the name of the Father, the Son and the Holy Spirit (Matthew 28:19). In Acts, believers in Samaria and Ephesus were baptized *into* the name of the Lord Jesus (Acts 8:16; 19:5). In Galatians 3:27, 'all of you who were baptised *into* Christ have clothed yourselves with Christ'. And it is just the same here: 'baptised *into* Christ'.

Baptism in the New Testament is a dramatic sacrament or ordinance. It indicates not just that God washes away our sin, not just that he gives us his Holy Spirit, but that he places us *into* Christ. The essence of the Christian life, as visibly signified in baptism, is that God by his sheer grace puts us, places us, grafts us *into* Christ Jesus.

Reflect on the joys and challenges of being united with Christ. Today, if you are going through deep trials, draw comfort from your union with him.

> What shall support us in that trying hour? . . . Nothing, nothing can do it but close communion with Christ. Christ dwelling in our hearts by faith – Christ putting His right arm under our heads – Christ felt to be sitting by our side – Christ can alone give us the complete victory in the . . . struggle.
>
> (J. C. Ryle, 'Sickness' in *Practical Religion: Being Plain Papers on the Daily Duties, Experience, Dangers, and Privileges of Professing Christians*, Charles Murray, 1900, pp. 372–374)

If you haven't been baptized, will you consider taking this step to signify that you are united with Christ and want to identify with him?

Day 9

Read Romans 6:1–7
Key verses: Romans 6:3–5

....

[3]Or don't you know that all of us who were baptised into Christ Jesus were baptised into his death? [4]We were therefore buried with him through baptism into death in order that, just as Christ was raised from the dead through the glory of the Father, we too may live a new life. [5]For if we have been united with him in a death like his, we will certainly also be united with him in a resurrection like his.

You are united with Christ. Don't imagine that this is some vague association or over-spiritualized language. We are not united to Jesus in any general sense; we must be more particular than that. The only Jesus Christ with whom we have been identified and made one is the Christ who died and rose again. So you and I have been united to Christ in his death and resurrection. The picture symbolism of baptism in verses 3–5 describes this union and its implications.

Baptism took place in the open air, in some stream or river. The individual would go down into the water – whether he or she was partially or totally immersed really does not matter! – where he or she would seem to be buried and then to rise again. Baptism would dramatize the individual's death, burial and resurrection to a new life. Baptism is a sort of funeral and resurrection from the grave as well.

So a Christian by faith inwardly, and by baptism outwardly, has been united to Christ in his death and resurrection. We have actually shared in the death and resurrection of Jesus. In fact, the day we came to know Christ was our funeral, the moment when we said 'goodbye' to our old life and began our new life in Christ.

Christianity doesn't just tinker around the edges of our life, promoting self-improvement. Our union with Christ marks a decisive change from our past. Are you living out the symbolism of your baptism or are you settling for mediocrity, something less than the gospel of Christ?

I would like to buy about three quid's worth of gospel, please. Not too much—just enough to make me happy, but not so much that I get addicted. I don't want so much gospel that I learn to really hate covetousness and lust. I certainly don't want so much that I start to love my enemies, cherish self-denial, and contemplate missionary service in some alien culture. I want ecstasy, not repentance; I want transcendence, not transformation. I would like to be cherished by some nice, forgiving, broad-minded people, but I myself don't want to love those from different races – especially if they smell. I would like enough gospel to make my family secure and my children well behaved, but not so much that I find my ambitions redirected or my giving too greatly enlarged. I would like about three quid's worth of gospel, please.

(D. A. Carson, *Basics for Believers: An Exposition of Philippians*, IVP, 2004, p. 9)

Day 10

Read Romans 6:5–10
Key verse: Romans 6:10

···

10 The death he died, he died to sin once for all; but the life he lives, he lives to God.

Some parts of the Bible are easy to understand (though perhaps harder to obey!). But how do we come to understand what more difficult passages mean? One fundamental principle of biblical interpretation is that the same phrase bears the same meaning in the same context. The phrase 'died to sin' occurs three times in this section. Twice it refers to Christians (verses 2, 11) and once it refers to Christ (verse 10); therefore we have to find an explanation which is true for Christ and of Christians.

When you die physically, your five senses cease to operate. You can no longer touch, see, smell, etc. Some people assume then that 'dead to sin' means we become unresponsive to sin. We became like a dead man so when temptation comes, we neither feel it nor react to it. But 'dead to sin' can't mean that Christ became unresponsive to sin, because he was never alive to sin in the first place. We also know that as Christians, we are not unresponsive to sin. Our fallen nature is alive and kicking! Why else would the Bible exhort us: 'do not let sin reign' (verse 12)? Chapter 8 urges us not to set our minds on the things of the flesh and in chapter 13:14, Paul says we are not to gratify the flesh. These would be absurd injunctions if the flesh was dead and had no desires.

In fact, in the Bible, death is spoken of not so much in physical terms but in moral and legal terms. Whenever sin and death are spoken of together in Scripture, the essential relation to them is that death is sin's penalty. From Genesis 2:17, disobedience is linked with death, right through to Revelation 21 where the destiny of sinners is 'the second death' (verse 8).

Death is to be understood as the just reward for sin (see Romans 1:32; 6:23). So Christ died to sin in the sense that he bore sin's penalty. He died for our sins, bearing them in his own innocent and sacred person. The death that Jesus died was the wages of our sin. He met sin's claim; he paid its penalty; he accepted its reward; and he did it once and for all. So sin had no more claim on him and he was raised from the dead to prove the satisfactoriness of his sin-bearing. He now lives forever unto God. In the same way, by our union with Christ, we have also died to sin. We have borne its penalty; it has no more claim on us.

Marvel at the scandal of God's grace. Christ took our place: he died the death we should have died.

> He was pierced for our transgressions,
>   he was crushed for our iniquities;
> the punishment that brought us peace was on him,
>   and by his wounds we are healed.
> (Isaiah 53:5–6)

> Bearing shame and scoffing rude,
> In my place condemned He stood;
> Sealed my pardon with His blood.
> Hallelujah! What a Saviour!
> (Philip P. Bliss, 'Hallelujah! What a Saviour!', 1875)

Day 11

Read Romans 6:5–10
Key verses: Romans 6:6–7

. . . .

> [6] *For we know that our old self was crucified with him so that the body ruled by sin might be done away with, that we should no longer be slaves to sin –* [7] *because anyone who has died has been set free from sin.*

We feel the pull of sin every day, so how can it be true that we are 'no longer . . . slaves to sin'?

Verse 6 says that the old self was crucified with Christ (stage 1), in order that the sinful body might be done away with (stage 2), so that we might no longer be slaves to sin (stage 3). To understand how the ultimate stage of being set free from sin happens, we must go back to stage 2. The 'body' does not refer to the human body; our body is not sinful in itself. The word refers to our sinful nature that needs to 'be done away with' so we no longer serve sin. The verb for 'to be done away with' is the same verb used in Hebrews 2:14 of the devil. It conveys the idea of being not extinct, but defeated. Not annihilated, but deprived of power. Our sinful nature is no more extinct than the devil, but God's will is that the dominion of both should be broken – and it has been.

How is our sinful nature going to be deprived of power? Go back to the first stage of Paul's argument. It is only possible because of the crucifixion of the old self. The 'old self' is not our old unregenerate nature; it is not the same as 'the body'. It is our old unregenerate life, the man or woman we once were. So what was crucified with Christ was not a part of me called my old nature, but the whole of me as I was before I was converted. My 'old self' is my pre-conversion life.

How is it that having been crucified with Christ and having 'died to sin' in the sense of bearing its penalty, we are delivered from the bondage of sin? Verse 7 gives the answer. The verb that is translated 'set free' is used twenty-five times in the New Testament, each time conveying the sense of being justified. We are freed from sin in the sense that we are justified from it; the penalty has been paid. We are like a convicted criminal who has served his sentence, and leaves the prison free. He has paid the penalty; the law no longer has anything against him, and he is now justified from his sin.

We shall be tempted by sin until the day we die. Satan will cajole us to go back to our old ways, try to convince us we can't resist sin's power, and accuse us of past failures. Don't believe the lies! Sin's penalty has been paid so its authority over you has been broken. Today, as you face opportunities to sin, ask for God's strength to stand firm and live out the freedom that Christ has won for us.

If the Son sets you free, you will be free indeed.
(John 8:36)

Day 12

Read Romans 6:8–14
Key verse: Romans 6:11

....

[11] In the same way, count yourselves dead to sin but alive to God in Christ Jesus.

We have got to become what we are. Paul has explained how we have died to sin but now he urges us to 'count yourselves dead to sin.' The RSV version says, 'consider yourselves'; the KJV version says, 'reckon . . . yourselves' as being what in fact we are, dead to sin and alive to God.

This is not make-believe. 'Reckoning' is not summoning our faith to believe something we do not believe. It is not pretending that our old nature has died, when we know it has not. It is to realize that our old self – that is, our former self – did die with Christ. Once we realize that our old life is ended, the score settled, the debt paid, the law satisfied, we shall want to have nothing more to do with it. It is finished.

Think of it in terms of a biography written in two volumes. One volume is the story of me before my conversion. The second volume is the story of me after I was made a new creation in Christ. We are simply called to reckon this – not to pretend it, but to realize it. It is a fact and we need to lay hold of it. We have to let our minds meditate on these truths until we grasp them firmly.

You see, the secret of holy living is in the mind. It is *knowing* that 'our old self was crucified with [Christ]' (verse 6). It is *knowing* that baptism into Christ is baptism into his death and resurrection (verse 3). It is *counting*, intellectually realizing, that in Christ we have died to sin and live for God (verse 11). Know these things, meditate on these things, reckon these things.

Can a Christian live as though he or she were still in his or her sins? I suppose it is not impossible. But it is utterly incongruous. It is like an adult returning to his or her childhood, a freed prisoner to his or her prison cell. By union with Christ, our whole status has changed. Our faith and baptism have cut us off irrevocably from the old life and committed us to the new. Our baptism stands between us and the old life as a door between two rooms. It has closed upon one room and has opened into another. We have died; we have risen. How can we live again in what we have died to?

Why must we count ourselves to be something we already are? Because being 'dead to sin' is like a privilege or legal right. Though it may be true or in force, a person might not realize or utilize the right/privilege. For example, you may have a trust fund put into your name, but unless you draw on it, it won't change your actual financial condition . . . So we must 'count ourselves dead to sin' because unless we act on this great privilege, it will not automatically be realized in our experience. We have to appropriate it, live it, enjoy it.

(Tim Keller, *Romans 1–7 For You*, Good Book Company, 2014, pp. 143–144)

Day 13

Read Romans 6:8–14
Key verses: Romans 6:12–13

• •

> [12] *Therefore do not let sin reign in your mortal body so that you obey its evil desires.* [13] *Do not offer any part of yourself to sin as an instrument of wickedness, but rather offer yourselves to God as those who have been brought from death to life; and offer every part of yourself to him as an instrument of righteousness.*

What should be the stand-out features of volume 2 of our biography? What behaviour should characterize our lives?

Paul advocates a two-pronged approach. First he gives us a negative charge: 'do not let sin reign' – do not let sin be your king, do not let it rule over you (verse 12). 'Do not offer' – do not go on yielding yourself, allowing sin to use you to further its unrighteous purposes (verse 13). Then he gives us a positive charge: 'offer yourselves to God' as those who are alive from the dead, which is precisely what you are. You have died to sin, bearing its penalty; you have risen again, alive from the dead; now yield yourselves to God. In other words, do not let sin be your king to rule over you; let God be your king to rule over you. Do not let sin be your lord, to use you in its service; let God be your Lord, to use you in his service.

Why yield ourselves to God and not to sin? Because we are alive from the dead (verse 13), so we are no longer under law, but under grace. God in grace has justified you in Christ; in Christ, sin's penalty is paid, and the law's demands are met. Neither sin nor the law has any further claim on you. You have been rescued from their tyranny. You have changed sides. You are no longer a prisoner of the law but a child of God, under his grace.

To know ourselves under grace and not under law, far from encouraging us to sin in order that grace may increase, actually weans us away from the world, the flesh and the devil (Ephesians 2:1–3). By grace we have opened a new volume in our biography, and there is no going back.

Living as a Christian does not simply mean avoiding sin. As Paul has explained, we need a two-pronged approach. We also need to be positively striving for holiness; offering every part of ourselves to God. What disciplines have you put in place to help you in this pursuit? How are you getting on? Are there areas where you need more grace-driven effort?

> If you want to be Christlike you need to have communion with Christ, and if you want communion with Christ you need to do it on his terms with the channels of grace he's provided [prayer, Bible reading, church fellowship, Lord's table]. And that means the only way to extraordinary holiness is through ordinary means.
> (Kevin DeYoung, *The Hole in Our Holiness*, Crossway Books, 2012, p. 135)

Day 14

Read Romans 6:15–23

Key verses: Romans 6:20–23

. . . .

[20]*When you were slaves to sin, you were free from the control of righteousness.* [21]*What benefit did you reap at that time from the things you are now ashamed of? Those things result in death!* [22]*But now that you have been set free from sin and have become slaves of God, the benefit you reap leads to holiness, and the result is eternal life.* [23]*For the wages of sin is death, but the gift of God is eternal life in Christ Jesus our Lord.*

'Gotta Serve Somebody' is the title of a famous Bob Dylan song. He was right. We like to think we're free, but in reality we all serve somebody. The Bible says we are either slaves to sin or slaves of God. Paul contrasts these two types of slavery. He highlights the differences:

- Beginning (verse 17)

  Our slavery to sin began at birth: 'you used to be slaves to sin.' We are slaves to sin by nature. But our slavery to God began by grace when we obeyed the gospel.

- Development (verse 19)

  The slavery of sin has as its result the grim process of a moral deterioration, but the slavery of God has as its result the glorious process of a moral sanctification. Each slavery develops; neither slavery stands still. In one we get better and better, and in the other we get worse and worse.

- End (verses 20–22)

  When we were slaves to sin the end was death, but now that we are slaves of God, the end is eternal life. Verse 23 sums it up: sin pays the wages we deserve, death, but God gives us a gift which we do not deserve, life.

Here then are two totally different lives, opposed to one another: the life of the old self and the new self. And they are two slaveries: by birth we are slaves to sin; by grace we have become the slaves of God. The slavery of sin yields no return except a moral deterioration and finally death. The slavery of God yields the precious return of sanctification and finally eternal life.

So you see the argument of verses 15–23 is that our conversion, this act of yielding or surrender to God, leads to a status of slavery, and slavery involves obedience.

In Old Testament times, every seven years, Hebrew slaves were set free from their masters. But just occasionally there was a slave who loved his master so much that he chose to commit himself to that master for life. The slave would go through a special ceremony to mark this commitment when his ear would be pierced with an awl (Exodus 21:2–6). Today, will you renew your commitment to be a slave of God? Are you willing to say, 'Pierce my ear, Lord. I want to be yours for life. Help me, by your grace, to be obedient to you and devoted to your service'?

Day 15

Read Romans 6:1–23
Key verses: Romans 6:15–17

....

15What then? Shall we sin because we are not under the law but under grace? By no means! 16Don't you know that when you offer yourselves to someone as obedient slaves, you are slaves of the one you obey – whether you are slaves to sin, which leads to death, or to obedience, which leads to righteousness? 17But thanks be to God that, though you used to be slaves to sin, you have come to obey from your heart the pattern of teaching that has now claimed your allegiance.

Sometimes we need to stand back from the details and take a look at the big picture. Today we'll take a bird's-eye view of chapter 6.

Both sections (verses 1–14 and verses 15–23) begin with virtually the same question: 'Shall we continue in sin?' Paul's critics, who intended to discredit the gospel, asked this. And it has been asked by enemies of the gospel ever since. Satan often whispers this question in our ear to entice us into sin: 'Why not continue in sin? God will forgive you. You are under grace. Go on. Do it again.'

How should we answer the devil? With the same outraged response as Paul: 'By no means!' (verses 2, 15). But we must go further than that and give a logical, irrefutable reason why the insinuations of the devil must be repudiated. Our answer is based on what we are. It is that we are one with Christ (verses 1–14) and we are slaves of God (verses 15–23). We became united to Christ by baptism, at least outwardly and visibly, and we became enslaved to God by the self-surrender of faith. But whether we emphasize the outward baptism or the inward faith, the point is the same. It is that our Christian conversion has had this result: it has united us to Christ, and it has enslaved us to God.

Now what we are has inescapable implications. If we are one with Christ – and we are – then with Christ we died to sin, and we live to God. If we are enslaved to God – which we are – then by that fact we are committed to obedience. It is inconceivable that we should wilfully persist in sin, presuming on the grace of God. The very thought is intolerable.

You and I need to be talking to ourselves, and saying, 'But don't you know that you are one with Christ; that you have died to sin, and risen to God? Don't you know that you are a slave to God, and committed therefore to obedience? Don't you know these things?' Go on asking yourself that question until you reply to yourself, 'Yes, I do know. And by the grace of God I shall live accordingly.'

Day 16

Read Romans 7:1–6
Key verse: Romans 7:6

....

⁶But now, by dying to what once bound us, we have been released from the law so that we serve in the new way of the Spirit, and not in the old way of the written code.

As Christians, do we need to obey the law that God gave Moses? Does it even apply to us?

Paul uses the illustration of marriage. A woman is only bound to her husband while he is alive. When he dies, she is free to marry again. His point is that just as death terminates a marriage, so death has terminated our bondage to the law. Of course it was Christ who died on the cross but, by our union with him, it is as if we have died and death has removed us altogether out of that sphere where the law exercises lordship. Using Paul's illustration, we were, so to speak, married to the law. Our obligation to obey the law was as binding as a marriage contract. But now we have been set free to marry Christ. Do you appreciate the intimacy of our union with Jesus Christ? Can you believe it? We are married, joined, to Christ.

But notice that this freedom from the law does not mean we are free to do what we please. We have another kind of bondage. We are free not to sin but to serve. And our new Christian slavery is literally 'in the new way of the Spirit, and not in the old way of the written code'. In the old covenant, the law was written on tablets of stone, but now the Holy Spirit writes the law in our hearts.

So is the law still binding upon the Christian? Yes and no! The law is not binding in the sense that our acceptance before God depends on it. Christ, in his death, has met the demands of the law, so it has no claim on us. But the law is still binding in the sense that our new life is still a bondage; we are still slaves. What has changed is the motive and means of our obedience. The motive: we don't obey the law because it is our master and we have to, but because Christ is our husband and we want to. The law says, 'Do this and you will live.' The gospel says, 'You live, so do this.' This means: we serve not by obeying an external code, but by surrendering to the indwelling Spirit. The Christian life is serving the risen Christ by the power of the indwelling Spirit.

Stop trying to undermine the value of Jesus' death by seeking to win God's approval through your works. Your relationship with God is not dependent on keeping all the rules or obeying the law. Jesus has met the demands of the law and you are justified. You are God's dearly beloved child. Serve him not to get his attention, nor to win his approval, but out of sheer gratefulness and joy for all that he has done for you. Try this burden on for size – it is much lighter to carry.

Day 17

Read Romans 7:7–13

Key verse: Romans 7:7

• •

⁷What shall we say, then? Is the law sinful? Certainly not! Nevertheless, I would not have known what sin was had it not been for the law.

Can you remember what you wanted to do the last time you saw a sign saying: 'Keep off the grass'? You may well have immediately wanted to walk on the grass! As soon as we are given a law we often want to do the opposite; we want to do what is forbidden. In the same way, as soon as we receive God's law, we sin. Does that mean I can blame God's law for my sin?

Paul is quick to respond: 'Certainly not!' He goes on to explain that the law itself is not sinful, but rather it:

- reveals sin (verse 7);

- provokes sin (verse 8) – the verb translated 'seizing the opportunity' is a military term for a springboard for offensive operations; sin found a foothold, an opportunity within us;

• condemns sin (verses 8–13) – when we try to live under the law's obligations, we die under its judgment.

Imagine a man caught red-handed committing a crime. He is arrested, brought to trial, found guilty and sent to prison. As he languishes in his cell, he is tempted to blame the law for his imprisonment. It is true that the law has condemned, convicted and sentenced him, but he has only himself to blame, because he committed the crime. And so Paul exonerates the law because although it reveals, provokes and condemns our sin, it cannot be held responsible for it.

The law itself is actually good (verse 12). The problem is our sin. It is our indwelling sin, our fallen nature, that explains the weakness of the law to save us. The law cannot save us for the simple reason that we cannot keep it, and we cannot keep it because of indwelling sin.

We don't like to admit our sin. Instead we often look around and blame everyone and everything else for our moral and spiritual failures. At times we even blame God and his commands for our dearth in holiness. Today, recognize the ugliness of your sin. Gaze on the cross and see your crucified Saviour. This is how much God abhors sin. We can't trifle with it or excuse it any longer. We need to hate sin as much as God does and deal with it in our lives.

> O Lord our God, grant us grace to desire Thee with our whole heart; that, so desiring, we may seek, and seeking find Thee; and so finding Thee may love Thee; and in loving Thee, may hate those sins from which Thou hast redeemed us.
>
> (St Anselm, ed. Martin H. Manser, *The Westminster Collection of Christian Quotations*, John Knox Press, 2001, p. 233)

Day 18

Read Romans 7:7–25
Key verses: Romans 7:14–15

••

14 We know that the law is spiritual; but I am unspiritual, sold as a slave to sin. 15 I do not understand what I do. For what I want to do I do not do, but what I hate I do.

Do you struggle daily with sin? Don't be surprised and don't despair! It is part of Christian living. Paul knew about this struggle. Bible-believing Christians have differing opinions, but my view is that verses 7–13 describe Paul's life before his conversion, and verse 14 onwards describes his present continuous conflict with sin. The fight is fierce and he refuses to accept defeat.

Some people resist the idea that a believer as mature as Paul would have to struggle with sin to such a degree. They prefer to read verses 14–25 as his pre-conversion experience. But look at the opinion he has of himself. Verse 18: 'I know that good itself does not dwell in me.'

Also verse 24: 'What a wretched man I am!' Only a mature believer thinks of himself like that! An unbeliever is characterized by self-righteousness and an immature believer by self-confidence; he or she doesn't ask, 'Who will rescue me?' Only a mature believer feels such disgust and despair when he or she sees his or her sinfulness. Notice also Paul's opinion of the law. He calls the law good (verse 16) and longs with all his being to obey it (verses 19, 22). That is not the language of an unbeliever.

In verses 7–13, Paul has shown that as an unbeliever he could not keep the law. From verse 14 onwards he shows that even as a Christian, by himself, he cannot keep God's law. His fallen human nature, which was his undoing before his conversion, leading him to sin and death, is still his undoing after his conversion – unless the power of the Holy Spirit subdues it (which he comes to in chapter 8).

We too need to honestly and humbly acknowledge our utter sinfulness. We shall never put our trust in the Holy Spirit until we despair of ourselves. We need to cry out, 'What a wretched person I am!' We need to reach that self-despair Paul experienced, because it is the first step on the road to holiness.

Contrary to popular belief, your struggle with sin is not going to get easier as you mature as a disciple. It is going to get harder, because the more of God's holiness you see, the more aware of your own sin you become. The light exposes the darkness. Thank God that in his kindness he reveals your sin and provides the means for obedience. Today, in God's strength, press on in your struggle against sin:

> Flee from all this [false teaching, love of money], and pursue righteousness, godliness, faith, love, endurance and gentleness. Fight the good fight of the faith. Take hold of the eternal life to which you were called when you made your good confession in the presence of many witnesses.
>
> (1 Timothy 6:11–12)

Day 19

Read Romans 7:14–25
Key verses: Romans 7:21–23

· ·

21 So I find this law at work: although I want to do good, evil is right there with me. 22 For in my inner being I delight in God's law; 23 but I see another law at work in me, waging war against the law of my mind and making me a prisoner of the law of sin at work within me.

When we want to emphasize a point in our emails or texts, we underline, use capital letters or change the font to bold. Here, Paul emphasizes the importance of his message by reiterating it in parallel sections.

Verses 14–17 and 18–20 both begin with a frank acknowledgment of our sin (verses 14, 18). Paul is aware that on his own he is a slave of sin, albeit a reluctant, resistant slave. Even as a Christian, he is brought into captivity and bondage by sin. Both sections continue with a vivid description of the resulting conflict. Christians who know, love and long to do the will of God, but who are not walking according to the Spirit, cannot do it. Because of their sinful nature, they cannot do what they want to do. So when they sin it is against their mind and will, and the whole tenor of their life. Both sections conclude that, apart from the Holy Spirit, sin means that obedience to God is impossible.

In verse 21, Paul sums up the general principle at work: 'although I want to do good, evil is right there with me.' There are two opposing forces at work: his mind and his flesh (verse 23). This is a real, bitter, unremitting conflict in every Christian's experience. Our mind is simply delighting in God's law, and longing to do it, but our flesh is hostile to it, and refuses to submit.

Paul's response? A cry of despair: 'What a wretched man I am! Who will rescue me from this body that is subject to death?' (verse 24). This is followed by a cry of triumph: 'Thanks be to God, who delivers me through Jesus Christ our Lord!' (verse 25). Both of these are the cries of a mature believer. We cry out because of the inner corruption of our sinful nature and we long for deliverance. But then we cry out in triumph because we know that God is the one and only deliverer. He is the one who gives us deliverance now through the Holy Spirit, and he is the one who on the last day, at the resurrection, will give us a new body, without any sin or corruption.

Praise God! He is our rescuer, our great deliverer:

> The LORD is my rock, my fortress and my deliverer;
>   my God is my rock, in whom I take refuge,
>   my shield and the horn of my salvation,
>   my stronghold.
> (Psalm 18:2)

> The Lord will rescue me from every evil attack and will bring me safely to his heavenly kingdom. To him be glory for ever and ever. Amen.
> (2 Timothy 4:18)

Day 20

Read Romans 7:25 – 8:4
Key verses: Romans 8:1–2

· ·

¹Therefore, there is now no condemnation for those who are in Christ Jesus, ²because through Christ Jesus the law of the Spirit who gives life has set you free from the law of sin and death.

Sin within us is like one of those tricky birthday candles that keeps reigniting when we think we've blown it out. (Christopher Ash, *Teaching Romans*, Christian Focus, 2009, p. 268)

I don't believe that the Christian ever passes once and for all out of Romans 7 and into Romans 8, out of the cry of despair and into the cry of victory. We are always crying out for deliverance and we are always exulting in our deliverer. Whenever we are made conscious of the power of indwelling sin, it is the same.

In verse 25, Paul sums up with beautiful lucidity this double servitude: 'I myself in my mind [we might say, with all my heart and soul] am a slave to God's law, but in my sinful nature [unless it is subdued by the Holy Spirit] a slave to the law of sin.' Whether we serve the law of God or the law of sin depends on whether our mind or our sinful nature is in control. And the question is: 'How can the mind gain ascendency over the flesh, our sinful nature?' That question brings us to chapter 8:1–4 and the ministry of the Holy Spirit. Although he has never been far away in the background of chapter 7, the Holy Spirit has not yet been named.

Chapter 8:1–4 views the same battle as chapter 7, but from a different perspective and with a different outcome. In chapter 7 the conflict is between my mind and the flesh: between what I want to do and what, in myself, I cannot do. But in chapter 8 the conflict is between the Spirit and the flesh. The Holy Spirit is coming to my rescue, allying himself with my mind, the renewed mind he has given me, and subduing the flesh. Whereas in chapter 7:22 the believer delights in the law of God but cannot do it in himself because of indwelling sin now, according to chapter 8:4 he not only delights in it, but actually fulfils the law of God, because of the indwelling Spirit.

The battle continues. The Holy Spirit lives within us but we can never say that we've 'dealt' with sin in a particular area of life because it keeps raising its head, usually when we least expect it. The enemy can attack anyone at any time. Christopher Ash (*Teaching Romans*, Christian Focus, 2009) cautions:

- the respectable and happily married business traveller against sexual temptation;
- the generous donor against becoming complacent in her giving;
- the hard-working person approaching retirement who does not suspect that laziness may be lurking around the corner;
- the prayer warrior who thinks he has his prayer life under control; and
- the melancholy believer prone to self-pity who thinks she has got over this and has it under control.

> Be alert and of sober mind. Your enemy the devil prowls around like a roaring lion looking for someone to devour.
> (1 Peter 5:8)

Day 21

Read Romans 8:1–4
Key verses: Romans 8:3–4

....

> ³*For what the law was powerless to do because it was weakened by the flesh, God did by sending his own Son in the likeness of sinful flesh to be a sin offering. And so he condemned sin in the flesh,* ⁴*in order that the righteous requirement of the law might be fully met in us, who do not live according to the flesh but according to the Spirit.*

Imagine a painter standing back to appreciate how all the details and nuances have come together in his completed work. Paul is doing something similar at the beginning of chapter 8. In verses 1–2, the apostle steps back and surveys the whole Christian landscape, portraying the two great blessings of salvation that we have in Christ. We are delivered from condemnation (verse 1) and delivered from the law of sin and its bondage (verse 2).

Verses 3–4 tell us how this salvation is made available to us. God has done what the law could not do. The law cannot sanctify, the law cannot justify, because we cannot obey it. But God has done it! Praise his name! Through the death of his Son he justifies us (verse 3), and through the power of the indwelling Spirit he sanctifies us (verse 4).

He delivers us from bondage by the Spirit, in order that the 'righteous requirement of the law might be fully met in us'. Notice that verse 4 teaches some major truths about holiness.

• Holiness is the purpose of the incarnation and the death of Christ.

  'God sent his Son' not only that we might be justified, but in order that the righteousness of the law might be fulfilled in us – in other words, that we might obey the law.

• Holiness is the righteousness of the law.

  Far from the law being abolished in the Christian life, it is God's purpose that its righteous requirement might be fulfilled in us.

• Holiness is the work of the Holy Spirit.

The righteousness of the law is only fulfilled in us if we walk according to the Spirit.

So the reason for holiness is the death of Christ; the nature of holiness is the righteousness of the law; and the means of holiness is the power of the Holy Spirit.

God wants you to be holy. Through faith He already counts you holy in Christ. Now He intends to make you holy with Christ. This is no optional plan, no small potatoes. God saved you to sanctify you. God is in the beautification business, washing away spots and smoothing out wrinkles. He will have a blameless bride. He promised to work in you; He also calls you to work out. 'The beauty of holiness' is first of all the Lord's (Ps. 29:2, KJV). But by His grace it can also be yours. (Kevin DeYoung, *The Hole in Our Holiness*, Crossway Books, 2012, p. 146)

Day 22

Read Romans 8:5–13
Key verse: Romans 8:5

....

> [5]*Those who live according to the flesh have their minds set on what the flesh desires; but those who live in accordance with the Spirit have their minds set on what the Spirit desires.*

It all starts in the mind. Ultimately our thoughts govern our behaviour. How we live, what the Bible sometimes calls our 'walk', depends on the focus of our mind, as Paul outlines in verse 5. To set our mind on what the flesh desires or what the Spirit desires means to occupy ourselves with the things of the flesh or the Spirit. It is a question of our preoccupations, the ambitions which compel us, and the interests which engross us – how we spend our time, money and energies, what we give ourselves to. That is what you set your mind on.

Verse 6 describes the result of these two outlooks. To set the mind on the flesh *is* death. Not it *'will be'*, it *is* now death because it leads to sin, and therefore to separation from God, which is death. To set your mind on the Spirit is life now because it leads to holiness, and so to continuing fellowship with God, which is life. It also brings peace. Peace with God which is life, and peace within ourselves which is integration and harmony. In contrast, there is no peace for the one whose mind is set on the flesh. That person is hostile to God, and will not submit to his law (verse 7).

So there are two categories of people. If we are in the flesh we set our minds on the things of the flesh, so we walk according to the flesh, and so we die. But if we are in the Spirit, we set our mind upon the things of the Spirit and so we walk according to the Spirit, and so we live. What we are governs how we think; how we think governs how we behave; and how we behave governs our relationship to God, death or life.

What is going on in your mind? What do you think most about? What are you feeding your mind with? Will you keep up the process of renewing your mind, focusing on the things of the Spirit, so that you will be transformed more and more into the likeness of Christ (Romans 12:2)?

[We] must understand that Christianity is not served by mindlessness, but by the knowledge of God through the Word of God. Such knowledge engages our minds, stirs our hearts, and transforms our lives. This knowledge is personal. How is it fostered? By listening to what He says (the priority of preaching), by engaging Him in conversation (the emphasis on prayer), by spending time in His company (the need for a devotional life), and by being with others who know Him too (the need for gathered worship). This knowledge is progressive and dynamic, not static. At the end of our journey, we should still be exclaiming with Paul: 'I want to know Christ' (1 Corinthians 2:2).

(Alistair Begg, *Made For His Pleasure*, Moody Press, 1996, p. 22)

Day 23

Read Romans 8:5–13
Key verses: Romans 8:9–10

• •

⁹You, however, are not in the realm of the flesh but are in the realm of the Spirit, if indeed the Spirit of God lives in you . . . ¹⁰But if Christ is in you, then even though your body is subject to death because of sin, the Spirit gives life because of righteousness.

What is the distinguishing mark of a Christian? What sets him or her apart from unbelievers? It is that the Christian is indwelt by the Holy Spirit. In chapter 7, verses 17 and 20, Paul talked about the sin which dwells in him. Now he focuses on the privilege of the Christian being indwelt with the Spirit, who subdues and controls sin. Notice in verses 9–10 that the Spirit of God and the Spirit of Christ are the same person. Similarly, to have the Spirit dwelling in us and having Christ dwell in us are the same thing.

So what difference does the indwelling Spirit make? Life! Verses 10–11 tell us that the Holy Spirit brings life for our spirits now and life for our bodies at the end. Because the Holy Spirit is the Spirit of life; he is the Lord, the life-giver. Although our bodies are mortal, our spirits are alive; the Holy Spirit has given them life. Because of Adam's sin we die physically, but because of Christ's righteousness we live spiritually. Our spirits are alive because Christ by his Spirit dwells in us and has given us life. And although at present it is only our spirits that live, on the last day our bodies are going to live as well, incorruptibly. The same Spirit which quickens our hearts now will quicken our bodies.

Paul concludes that we are debtors (verse 12, KJV). He breaks off before completing the sentence, but the implication is that we are debtors to the Holy Spirit. If the Spirit has given life to our spirits, then we must put to death the deeds of the body so that we may continue to live the life that the Spirit has given us. So we have an obligation to holiness. We have an obligation to live up to our Christian status and privilege, and to do nothing that is inconsistent with the life of the Spirit that is in us, but rather to nourish and foster this life.

We are debtors to the Holy Spirit, debtors to God for all the grace he has shown us. Today, pray for God's help to live up to your true status and privilege.

O to grace how great a debtor
Daily I'm constrained to be!
Let Thy goodness, like a fetter,
Bind my wandering heart to Thee.
Prone to wander, Lord, I feel it,
Prone to leave the God I love;
Here's my heart, O take and seal it,
Seal it for Thy courts above.
(Robert Robinson, 'Come Thou Fount of Every Blessing', 1759)

Day 24

Read Romans 8:5–13
Key verse: Romans 8:13

••

13 For if you live according to the flesh, you will die; but if by the Spirit you put to death the misdeeds of the body, you will live.

Most of us like to settle our debts. But how are we going to settle our debt to the Holy Spirit? If we are going to be honourable and discharge our debt, there will be two processes involved: mortification and aspiration.

Mortification, putting to death the deeds of the body, means a ruthless rejection of all practices we know to be wrong. It involves a daily repentance, turning from every known sinful habit, practice, association or thought. It is cutting out the eye, cutting off the hand, cutting off the foot, if temptation comes to us through what we see or do, or where we go. The only attitude we can adopt to the flesh is to kill it.

Aspiration, setting the mind on the things of the Spirit, is a wholehearted giving of ourselves in thought, energy and ambition, to whatever things are true and honest, just and pure, lovely and of good report. In order to give our mind to the things of the Spirit, we will need a disciplined use of the means of grace – prayer, reading and meditation on Scripture, fellowship, worship, the Lord's Supper and so on.

In both cases, mortification and aspiration, the verbs are in the present tense, because they are attitudes to be adopted, which are then constantly and unremittingly maintained. We are to keep putting to death the deeds of the body, or as Jesus said, 'take up [your] cross daily and follow me' (Luke 9:23–24). We are to keep setting our minds on the things of the Spirit, daily. These are the secrets of life in the fullest sense. There is no true life without the death called mortification and there is no true life without the discipline called aspiration. To sum up: it is as we mortify the flesh in the power of the Holy Spirit and set our minds on the things of the Spirit that the Spirit himself subdues our flesh.

We talk flippantly of carrying our cross when we refer to dealing with difficult relatives or a minor health issue. When a person carried a cross-beam through the streets in the first century it meant one thing: they were on their way to their execution. Jesus doesn't pull any punches when he describes discipleship. It is a daily – minute-by-minute in fact – putting to death of our agenda and programmes, our sinful flesh, and a yielding to him.

Imagine carrying your cross into your work meeting, as you care for your elderly relative, serve in church, study for exams, speak to non-Christian family members or look after young children. Feel the weight of the cross.

Now, at this point in your life, what does it mean to 'take up your cross daily and follow' Christ?

Day 25

Read Romans 8:12–17
Key verses: Romans 8:14, 17

••

14 For those who are led by the Spirit of God are the children of God . . . 17 Now if we are children, then we are heirs – heirs of God and co-heirs with Christ, if indeed we share in his sufferings in order that we may also share in his glory.

Most unbelievers would assume that if there is a God, surely we are all his children. Paul makes a sobering statement that not all human beings are God's children. Verse 14 definitely and deliberately limits this status to those who are being led by the Spirit, who are being enabled by the Spirit to walk along the narrow road of righteousness. To be led by the Spirit and to be a child of God are synonymous.

When we were converted, we received the Spirit of sonship or adoption. The Holy Spirit given to us when we believe makes us sons and daughters, not slaves. He does not recall us to the old slavery spoiled by fear. He grants us a new relationship in which we can approach God as our Father; more than that, he assures us of the status that he brings us. When we cry out, 'Abba, Father' (the very words that the Lord Jesus used in intimate prayer to God), it is the Holy Spirit bearing witness with our spirits that we are children of God. It is in our access to God in prayer that we sense our filial relationship to God, and we know ourselves the children of God. In prayer, the Holy Spirit bears witness to our spirit that we are God's children.

As God's children we are heirs, indeed co-heirs with Christ (verse 17). If we share his sonship, we shall share his inheritance in glory, but notice that if we share his glory, we must first share his sufferings. Suffering is the pathway to glory for Christ and for us. So we share his sufferings, his sonship and his glory. Indeed, the whole of the Christian life is identification with Christ.

See what great love the Father has lavished on us, that we should be called children of God!
(1 John 3:1)

We can call the Almighty God 'Our Father'. This sets Christianity apart from all the other religions of the world. Other religions invite us to worship and placate their gods, but Jesus came so that we could be adopted into God's family, so that we could relate to God in a personal way. As God's dearly loved child, come to him in prayer often, delight to spend time with him and bring him pleasure by the obedience of your life. Submit to his discipline knowing that he only wants the best for you; that is Christ's likeness formed in you. In times of suffering rest in him; find your comfort and strength in his Word.

If you struggle with assurance that you are part of God's family, come to him in prayer today and let the Holy Spirit minister this truth to your soul.

(See also John 1:12–13; Galatians 3:26–29; 4:4–7; Hebrews 12:4–11; 1 John 3:2, 10.)

Day 26

Read Romans 8:18–27
Key verses: Romans 8:20–21

....

20 For the creation was subjected to frustration, not by its own choice, but by the will of the one who subjected it, in hope 21 that the creation itself will be liberated from its bondage to decay and brought into the freedom and glory of the children of God.

Can you imagine what future glory will be like? Paul does not leave us wondering: 'I consider that our present sufferings are not worth comparing with the glory that will be revealed in us' (verse 18). Paul knew all about suffering (2 Corinthians 11:23–28), he knew that we would suffer as Jesus' disciples (Romans 8:17), and yet his conviction was that our present suffering is a drop in the ocean compared to the future glory that we shall experience.

Paul proves his claim by explaining that the glory we are waiting for is so great that even creation is longing for it. He lifts our heads up from our suffering and gives us a cosmic view. As nature has shared man's curse (Genesis 3), so nature now shares man's tribulation, and is going to share in man's glory. 'For the creation waits in eager expectation [as if standing on tiptoe with eager longing] for the children of God to be revealed' (Romans 8:19). Creation is waiting for this because this is the time when it too will be redeemed.

Creation is mentioned four times in verses 19–22, once in every verse. And notice how its present sufferings are described. It was subject to *frustration* (verse 20) not by its own will but by God's will. It is held in *bondage to decay* (verse 21), and it is *groaning* in pain (verse 22). Frustration is the same word that is translated 'vanity' in the Greek version of the Book of Ecclesiastes. The whole creation has been subjected to vanity. This frustration is explained as a bondage to decay – a continuous process in the universe that appears to be running down. And this process is, whether literally or metaphorically, accompanied by pain.

But the present suffering of creation, nature, is only temporary. There is hope of future glory – from bondage to freedom, from decay to glory incorruptible. Just as we are going to share Christ's glory, creation is going to share ours. The groans and pains that creation endures now are like the pains of childbirth (verse 22). In other words, they are not meaningless or purposeless pains; they are pains necessarily experienced in the bringing to birth of a new order.

When Paul talks about 'glory', he is not talking about your individual place in heaven. God's vision is far more magnificent and expansive. Creation is craning its neck in eager anticipation of the day when our transformation is complete and we, perfectly like Christ, are ruling a redeemed and restored new creation. That's glory!

Today, lift your head up from your suffering and enjoy Paul's cosmic view. Cling on to this certain hope that soon your suffering will give way to glory. Also, accept the challenge: if the groans of creation are not death throes but birth pains, rethink your stewardship of God's world. How could you better look after the resources that God has entrusted to our care?

Day 27

Read Romans 8:18–27
Key verse: Romans 8:23

∙∙

[23] Not only so, but we ourselves, who have the first-fruits of the Spirit, groan inwardly as we wait eagerly for our adoption to sonship, the redemption of our bodies.

We groan because of the ravages that sin makes in our lives, and in the lives of those we love . . . We groan in disappointment, in bereavement, in sorrow. We groan physically in our pain and our limitation. Life consists of a great deal of groaning.
(Ray Stedman, *From Guilt to Glory, vol.1*, Word, 1981, p. 241)

Our bodies are weak, fragile and mortal, subject to tiredness, sickness, pain and death (2 Corinthians 5), and they are indwelt by sin. Physical frailty and our fallen nature cause us to groan and long for future glory. On that last day we are going to be given new, redeemed, resurrection bodies, without sin. But there's more. Future glory is also about our 'adoption'. In one sense we have already received our adoption, but in another sense we are still waiting. We are God's children but we are not yet conformed, in either body or character, to Christ. Neither has our sonship been publicly recognized or revealed. This will happen on the last day (verse 19).

How can we be sure of this glorious inheritance? We have the first fruits of the Holy Spirit (verse 23). The Holy Spirit is the guarantee and foretaste of our full inheritance. Sometimes Paul uses a business metaphor and describes the Holy Spirit as the first instalment, the down payment, which certifies that the remainder is going to be paid later (2 Corinthians 1:22). Here he uses a farming metaphor. The first fruits of the harvest are a pledge of the full crop to come. So the Holy Spirit not only makes us children of God as the Spirit of adoption; he not only witnesses with our spirit that we are children of God; he himself is the pledge of our complete adoption to be the sons of God when our bodies are redeemed. In the meantime, we wait patiently for future glory (verse 25).

Are you groaning today, overwhelmed by circumstances, frustrated by sin? You don't need to groan in despair or doubt, because we have a sure hope. We groan as adopted children longing for our Father to usher in his promised future. Like creation, be on tiptoes eagerly awaiting your deliverance: the day your sinful body will be done away with. You will see Christ and experience the fullness of your salvation.

In the meantime, wait. Wait with endurance, bearing up under all sorts of trials, because you have hope in God. Also wait patiently because you are confident in God's promise that the first fruits will be followed by the harvest.

> For the grace of God has appeared that offers salvation to all people. It teaches us to say 'No' to ungodliness and worldly passions, and to live self-controlled, upright and godly lives in this present age, while we wait for the blessed hope – the appearing of the glory of our great God and Saviour, Jesus Christ.
> (Titus 2:11–13)

Day 28

Read Romans 8:18–27
Key verses: Romans 8:26–27

. . . .

26 In the same way, the Spirit helps us in our weakness. We do not know what we ought to pray for, but the Spirit himself intercedes for us through wordless groans. 27 And he who searches our hearts knows the mind of the Spirit, because the Spirit intercedes for God's people in accordance with the will of God.

Do you struggle to pray? Often we find it hard to settle down to pray and then, when we do, we get distracted! At other times we just don't know what words to say.

Helping us in our prayer life is another ministry that the Holy Spirit fulfils. He is mentioned four times in these two verses. We don't often talk about the Holy Spirit's role in prayer, yet we are taught in the Bible that our access to God is not only through the Son, but by the Spirit. The Holy Spirit's inspiration is as necessary as the Son's mediation in our access to God in prayer. Here Paul is talking specifically about our ignorance in prayer. When we don't know precisely what to pray for as we ought, the Holy Spirit helps us in our weakness.

Sometimes when believers don't know how to pray in words, they groan. Sometimes we groan because of the intensity of our longing. At other times we are so burdened by our own mortality, or by our sin, that we can only groan. But what J. B. Phillips calls 'those agonising longings which never find words' (Romans 8:26) are not to be despised, as if we ought to be able to put them into language. On the contrary, when we sigh with inarticulate desires, it is the Holy Spirit himself interceding on our behalf, prompting these groans. We do not need to be ashamed of these wordless prayers. God the Father understands prayers that are sighed rather than said, because he searches our hearts. He can read our hearts and our thoughts and he knows what is the mind of the Spirit, because the Holy Spirit always prays in accordance with the will of God. And so the Father in heaven answers the prayers prompted by the Spirit in our hearts.

There are times when we struggle to pray. When we are lying in a hospital bed too ill to speak; when someone we love is suffering so intensely that we are too numb to articulate our thoughts; when we are not sure if we should be asking God to relieve us of our suffering or give us the strength to endure it. But our inability to pray doesn't stop God's will unfolding in our lives. In those times, God the Holy Spirit carries our prayers to God the Father. And he always knows what to pray for because he knows God's will. How amazing that God prays to God on our behalf! And not only that, we have two intercessors: Jesus in heaven (Romans 8:34) and the Holy Spirit in our hearts, both praying to God the Father for us. Surely we are greatly loved.

Day 29

Read Romans 8:28–39
Key verses: Romans 8:28–30

• •

28 And we know that in all things God works for the good of those who love him, who have been called according to his purpose. 29 For those God foreknew he also predestined to be conformed to the image of his Son, that he might be the firstborn among many brothers and sisters. 30 And those he predestined, he also called; those he called, he also justified; those he justified, he also glorified.

What is the best-known verse in the Bible? A few vie for first position, but Romans 8:28 surely must come close. Many Christians have taken comfort from the fact that God works all things together for good – including the pains and the groans of the previous paragraphs – for those who love him and are 'called according to his purpose'.

In verses 29–30, Paul sets out five affirmations which explain what is meant by the divine calling, and in what sense God works all things together for good. These affirmations explain God's purpose in saving sinners. First he foreknew and second he predestined. The difference between foreknowledge and predestination is, perhaps, that God's electing choice was formed in his mind before he willed it. His decision preceded his decree. The implication clearly is that everyone who is saved can ascribe each stage of his or her salvation not to his or her merit or obedience, but only to God's favour and action. Notice that the purpose of God's predestination is not favouritism but holiness, Christlikeness.

The third affirmation is that God called; and the fourth is that he justified. The call of God is the historical outworking of his eternal predestination, and those whom God calls respond in faith to the call. And those who believe, God justifies, accepting them in Christ as his own. Fifth, he glorified, bringing them to resurrection and to heaven, with new bodies in a new world. So certain is this final stage of glorification that it is expressed in the aorist tense as if it were past, like the other four stages which *are* past.

These five affirmations are like a chain with five un-breakable links. God is pictured as moving on steadily from stage to stage, from an eternal foreknowledge and predestination, through to a historical call and justification, to a final glorification of his people in heaven.

When we say, 'All things work together for good', we don't mean that life will always turn out as we'd like, that healing will come or a difficult situation will turn around. Rather, it means we can have great confidence that in God's sovereignty, he will use everything that happens to us in life for our good. The 'good' that Paul is talking about is our ultimate good, that one day we will be conformed to the image of Christ. So whatever is happening in your life right now, whatever struggles you are dealing with, you can be sure that God will finish his work in you. You will be glorified, and your eternal destiny is secure.

Day 30

Read Romans 8:28–39
Key verses: Romans 8:38–39

• •

38 For I am convinced that neither death nor life, neither angels nor demons, neither the present nor the future, nor any powers, 39 neither height nor depth, nor anything else in all creation, will be able to separate us from the love of God that is in Christ Jesus our Lord.

In our suffering, when our own faith falters and the world is full of insecurity, can we be sure of God's love?

Paul responds by asking five questions.

• 'If God is for us, who can be against us?' (verse 31)

If he'd simply asked, 'Who can be against us?', we could have come up with a long list! Unbelievers, indwelling sin, death and the devil all oppose us. But Paul's question is, 'If the God who foreknew, predestined, called, justified and glorified us is for us, who can be against us?' Our enemies may set themselves against us, but they can never prevail if God is on our side.

- 'He who did not spare his own Son, but gave him up for us all – how will he not also, along with him, graciously give us all things?' (verse 32)

If Paul had simply asked, 'Will God not give us all things?', we might have wondered. But Paul banishes any lingering doubts. God has already given us his Son: 'with this gift how can he fail to lavish upon us all he has to give?' (NEB). The cross proves the generosity of God.

- 'Who will bring any charge against those whom God has chosen?' (verse 33)

We are in a court of law. If the question had been, 'Who will bring any charge against us?', we might well answer: my conscience and the devil (Revelation 12:10). But the devil's accusations fall to the ground; they do not hurt us. They are like arrows off a shield because we are God's chosen, whom he has justified. And if God has justified us, no accusation can stand against us.

- 'Who then is the one who condemns?' (verse 34)

Our critics, all the demons in hell and even our own hearts seek to condemn us (1 John 3:20–21). But their threats are idle. Jesus died for the sins which should have condemned us. His resurrection proves that the penalty for sin has been paid in full.

- 'Who shall separate us from the love of Christ?' (verse 35)

Verses 35–39 list all the perilous and painful things that could separate us from the love of God. But far from separating us from Christ's love, in the experience and enduring of these sufferings, 'we are more than conquerors' (verse 37). The Greek word conveys the idea of being 'super-conquerors'. These adversities cannot separate us from Christ's love because we conquer in them through him who has proved his love at the cross. Christ has proved his love by his sufferings, so our sufferings cannot separate us from his love.

There is nothing that you will go through today – or in the coming days – that can separate you from God's love: no broken romance, financial hardship, tragedy or even death. Although at times your hold on God may be frail, he has you in his grip and will not let you go. God loves you and is for you. Hold fast to this unshakeable conviction: live in the confidence, comfort and joy of it.

For further study

If you would like to do further study on Romans, the following books may be useful.

- F. F. Bruce, *Romans* (Tyndale New Testament Commentaries) (IVP, 2008)

- Kent Hughes, *Romans: Righteousness from Heaven* (Preaching the Word) (Crossway, 1991)

- Douglas Moo, *Epistle to the Romans* (New International Commentary on the New Testament) (Eerdmans, 1996)

- Thomas Schreiner, *Romans* (Baker Exegetical Commentary on the New Testament) (Baker, 1998)

- John Stott, *The Message of Romans* (Bible Speaks Today) (IVP, 1994)

KESWICK MINISTRIES

Our purpose

Keswick Ministries is committed to the spiritual renewal of God's people for his mission in the world.

God's purpose is to bring his blessing to all the nations of the world. That promise of blessing, which touches every aspect of human life, is ultimately fulfilled through the life, death, resurrection, ascension and future return of Christ. All of the people of God are called to participate in his missionary purposes, wherever he may place them. The central vision of Keswick Ministries is to see the people of God equipped, encouraged and refreshed to fulfil that calling, directed and guided by God's Word in the power of his Spirit, for the glory of his Son.

Our priorities

Keswick Ministries seeks to serve the local church through:

- *Hearing God's Word*: the Scriptures are the foundation for the church's life, growth and mission, and Keswick Ministries is committed to preaching and teaching God's Word in a way that is faithful to Scripture and relevant to Christians of all ages and backgrounds.

- *Becoming like God's Son*: from its earliest days the Keswick movement has encouraged Christians to live godly lives in the power of the Spirit, to grow in Christ-likeness and to live under his lordship in every area of life. This is God's will for his people in every culture and generation.

- *Serving God's mission*: the authentic response to God's Word is obedience to his mission, and the inevitable result of Christlikeness is sacrificial service. Keswick Ministries seeks to encourage committed discipleship in family life, work and society, and energetic engagement in the cause of world mission.

Our ministry

- *Keswick: the event.* Every summer the town of Keswick hosts a three-week convention, which attracts some 15,000 Christians from the UK and around the world. The event provides Bible teaching for all ages, vibrant worship, a sense of unity across generations and denominations, and an inspirational call to serve Christ in the world. It caters for children of all ages and has a strong youth and young adult programme. And it all takes place in the beautiful Lake District – a perfect setting for rest, recreation and refreshment.

- *Keswick: the movement.* For 140 years the work of Keswick has had an impact on churches worldwide, and today the movement is underway throughout the UK, as well as in many parts of Europe, Asia, North America, Australia, Africa and the Caribbean. Keswick Ministries is committed to strengthening the network in the UK and beyond, through prayer, news, pioneering and cooperative activity.

- *Keswick resources.* Keswick Ministries produces a range of books and booklets based on the core foundations of Christian life and mission. It makes Bible teaching available through free access to mp3 downloads, and the sale of DVDs and CDs. It broadcasts online through Clayton TV and annual BBC Radio 4 services.

- *Keswick teaching and training.* In addition to the summer convention, Keswick Ministries is developing teaching and training events that will happen at other times of the year and in other places.

Our unity

The Keswick movement worldwide has adopted a key Pauline statement to describe its gospel inclusivity: 'for you are all one in Christ Jesus' (Galatians 3:28). Keswick Ministries works with evangelicals from a wide variety of church backgrounds, on the understanding that they share a commitment to the essential truths of the Christian faith as set out in its statement of belief.

Our contact details
T: 01768 780075
E: info@keswickministries.org
W: www.keswickministries.org
Mail: Keswick Ministries, Rawnsley Centre, Main Street, Keswick, Cumbria CA12 5NP, England

Related titles from IVP

Food for the Journey

The Food for the Journey series offers daily devotionals from well-loved Bible teachers at the Keswick Convention in an ideal pocket-sized format – to accompany you wherever you go.

Available in the series

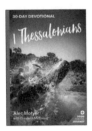

1 Thessalonians

Alec Motyer with
Elizabeth McQuoid
978 1 78359 439 9

2 Timothy

Michael Baughen with
Elizabeth McQuoid
978 1 78359 438 2

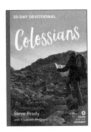

Colossians

Steve Brady with
Elizabeth McQuoid
978 1 78359 722 2

Ezekiel

Liam Goligher with
Elizabeth McQuoid
978 1 78359 603 4

Habakkuk

Jonathan Lamb with
Elizabeth McQuoid
978 1 78359 652 2

Hebrews

Charles Price with
Elizabeth McQuoid
978 1 78359 611 9

James

Stuart Briscoe with
Elizabeth McQuoid
978 1 78359 523 5

John 14 – 17

Simon Manchester with
Elizabeth McQuoid
978 1 78359 495 5

Available from your local Christian bookshop or **www.ivpbooks.com**

Food for the Journey

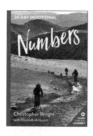   

Numbers

Christopher Wright
with Elizabeth
McQuoid
978 1 78359 720 8

Revelation

Paul Mallard with
Elizabeth McQuoid
978 1 78359 712 3

Romans 5 - 8

John Stott with
Elizabeth McQuoid
978 1 78359 718 5

Ruth

Alistair Begg with
Elizabeth McQuoid
978 1 78359 525 9

Praise for the series

'This devotional series is biblically rich,
theologically deep and full of wisdom . . .
I recommend it highly.' **Becky Manley Pippert,**
speaker, author of *Out of the Saltshaker and
into the World* and creator of the Live/Grow/
Know course and series of books

'These devotional guides are excellent tools.'
**John Risbridger, Minister and Team Leader,
Above Bar Church, Southampton**

'These bite-sized banquets . . . reveal our
loving Father weaving the loose and messy
ends of our everyday lives into his beautiful,
eternal purposes in Christ.' **Derek Burnside,
Principal, Capernwray Bible School**

'I would highly recommend this series of
30-day devotional books to anyone seeking
a tool that will help [him or her] to gain a
greater love of scripture, or just simply . . .
to do something out of devotion. Whatever
your motivation, these little books are a must-
read.' **Claud Jackson,** *Youthwork* **Magazine**

Available from your local Christian bookshop or **www.ivpbooks.com**

Related teaching CD and DVD packs

CD PACKS

1 Thessalonians
SWP2203D (5-CD pack)

2 Timothy
SWP2202D (4-CD pack)

Colossians
SWP2318D (4-CD pack)

Ezekiel
SWP2263D (5-CD pack)

Habakkuk
SWP2299D (5-CD pack)

Hebrews
SWP2281D (5-CD pack)

James
SWP2239D (4-CD pack)

John 14 - 17
SWP2238D (5-CD pack)

Numbers
SWP2317D (5-CD pack)

Revelation
SWP2300D (5-CD pack)

Roman 5 - 8
SWP2316D (4-CD pack)

Ruth
SWP2280D (5-CD pack)

Available from www.essentialchristian.com

Related teaching CD and DVD packs

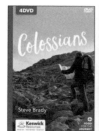

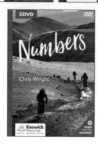

Colossians
SWP2318A (4-DVD pack)

Ezekiel
SWP2263A (5-DVD pack)

Habakkuk
SWP2299A (5-DVD pack)

John 14 - 17
SWP2238A (5-DVD pack)

Numbers
SWP2317A (5-DVD pack)

Revelation
SWP2300A (5-DVD pack)

Ruth
SWP2280A (5-DVD pack)